A Beautiful Mess

Sierrah Chavis

BookLeaf Publishing

Presentation by *BookLeaf Publishing*

Web: www.bookleafpub.com

E-mail: info@bookleafpub.com

ISBN: 9789357440202

First edition 2023

This book is dedicated to my three daughters, Honure, Grace and Reign, my husband and my dearest mother. My mother inspired me to write as she is a wonderful poet and writer. From an early age she used her writing to express her emotions and the way she was feeling. Her writing provokes healing, love and passion. My legacy is to pass my love for writing and poetry to my daughters and to help them understand the power of words. Lastly, to my husband thank you for always encouraging my writing and for allowing me to be the best version of myself everyday.

ACKNOWLEDGEMENT

We are all writers, because we are storytellers and humans tell the greatest stories. Don't be afraid to unleash the story that is living deep within you. it's time to release your message so you walk into your purpose.

Purpose

I see the vision but struggle with purpose.
I have dreams that haven't yet come true.
Because I struggle with my purpose.
I see plans for my future.
But yet I struggle with the idea of seeing it
through.
I seek and I find.
I find and I seek.
The more i see the more I seek.
But is it my purpose.
or some idea I've found to be intriguing.
I've found lots of things to inspire me.
Looking for the right thing to set me up.
But yet I'm lost in the mix of it all.
My purpose is defined for me but what if I fail
searching for it all.

all I want

We want it all yet all isn't what we want at all.
I want love but can't afford to be in love.
I want it all until all cost me.
Am I ready to put it all on the line.
Is love really blind or an illusion of my mind.
I want it all.
But what if all isn't what I need.
I want the car, house, money and family.
But at what cost.
Am I satisfied with it all.
or am I fixated with the idea.
that had it all.
More money more problems.
Everything that glitters ain't gold.
Because we hold onto the image of what feels
good instead of the reality or what isn't good for
you at all.

sense of belonging

Out of placed
Unsure of my sense of belonging
Where do I fit in at
Or do I fit at all
It's a piece of the puzzle missing and I can't
figure out where I belong
I'm trying to find my place
Make my voice loud and proud
But yet my mind races back
If I even fit at all
I'm not weak
I'm strong
So why do I feel like I don't belong
I have what it takes
Or am I delusional and wrong
Am I hoping for something that never belonged

Self-Image

Mirrors all around me
Only thing I see is broken glass
Do I fear what's looking back at me
Or am I fearless or fearful of what I can be
Am I avoiding the unfamiliar parts of me
Or trying to live up to something I cannot be
The image I hold up is of someone I want to be
I am driven by the image I use to be
But that person is me
I've aged, yes but deep down inside of me is
who I want to be
It's me
The image of myself no longers linger in mind
of the broken pieces from the glass
because I am taking care of the image I used to
be
She is me and I am content with the person I
want to be.

Peace

peace be with me, peace be still.
The silence sometimes scares me
Am I daydreaming or is it a feeling that's real.
i've sacrificed myself all for what.
peace is what I need.
But peace isn't free.
it comes with a sacrifice.
that I'm not willing to feel
peace is what I need in order to be free.
i'm free because I have peace.
peace be with me.

I stand

here I stand naked and all
I feel vulnerable and live in fear of what you
might say
my broken pieces are like glass
that can't be replaced
but i stand before you free from it all
no longer broken but
fulfilling my purpose
walking into my destiny
because I deserve it all.
i am no longer living in fear
because of what i cannot control
but i will walk with dignity because i know
i am way more
i stand with my head held high like I know i
belong.

Girl like me

Girl like me
Would you believe
Struggles with her identity
Fitting in was not easy
Not to be accepted by a race you most closely
identify with
Fair skin
Light skin
Your skin doesn't fit in
What are you
They said without hesitation
You don't fit in
You fear walking in a room
At what people might say about you
because you still struggle with your identity
Identify me as being strong
Yet when I walk in a room
Why do I feel so weak
Because for me my identity is still unknown
But I wanted to be accepted.
But I fear being wrong.

Mother's love

Holding you close to my heart
The feeling was so right
I don't want to let this moment go
God knew that I needed you and that you needed
me
My life isn't the same without you
Every pain I endured to bring you here
Was worth the fight
Your smile shines so bright
Like a warm sunny day the skies are just as blue
as your eyes reflect what's looking back at you
And your soul is just as sweet and kind
The memories we share are stored forever in a
keepsake
I am who I am because of the love you bring to
me each day. I will always hold you close to my
heart

Imprint

Your tiny hands leave an imprint of hope, love
and sacrifice.
Wherever you go
Whoever you represent
People will remember your imprint
Your love is graceful
Your love is constant
It does not seek validation
But a formation
of respect
Unity
And communication
When my feet enter the room
It commands attention
My head is held high
As I speak in a manner
That many can't even imagine.

Soulful

Charismatic
Sensational
Her soul was soulful and beautiful
Like a warm sunset over the ocean wave
She fell deeply in love
She would do anything for it
Even Giving up her soul
All for the name of love
She is nameless because the thought of
embracing
Her truth scares her

before i let go

One more thing before you go
Watch me grow into something i didn't know
You left me feeling blue
You thought i would be lost without you
But the joke is on you
But before i let you go
You must know
That i don't blame you
For what you couldn't do
I'm more than happy
So watch me grow into something new

dance

dance dance dance
Like you just received good news
Reclaim your sense of peace
Even when you don't feel anew
Because this all you
Can't nobody stop you from feeling the beat that
lives within your feet
So dance for you
Because you deserve to feel brand new
Don't worry about what people say they just
mad because they ain't you

secret

Sshsh
Don't tell no one
What I'm about to tell you will blow even your
mind
How much longer do we have to live in secrecy
I feel borrowed and used for holding on to your
little dark secret
Yeah I'm brand new because I'm tired of
holding back from the truth
Your secret is no longer my problem
I'm not holding back for the sake of our
relationship
because that died a long time ago
When you asked me to hold onto your little
Secret

freedom

To be who you are and to live the way you want
if we were all free to do as we wanted without
judgment or fear
words and beliefs will not be misconstrued.
Free from the shame that I love who I love but
people judge without cause
or reason all because you want to be free.
guilty because you want to please the people
who will always have an opinion regardless if
you are free or not.
She, Her, They, Them, but my pronoun is me.
I want to be free from it all
but there's a cost to live
whether we realize it at all
we all just want to be free

tears I've cried

Oh I've cried
Some of joy
Some of sadness
Some of fear
Some are mad
Some are glad
The tears I've cried
Provided me strength
I didn't know I had
In times of doubt
I relied on the tears I've cried
To lift me up
My cries provided me an armor for life
I'm not weak because I've cried
I'm stronger because I can

undo

I can't unsee
I can't unhear
I can't undo
What's done is done
But I refuse to live in fear
And with regret
The past will try to confine you
Leave you in despair
Frustrated that you become isolated in pain
Release it and don't try to undo what's already
been done
Move forward and become a better you
Focus on your progress and how far you've
come

world peace

What if we lived in a world where guns didn't
kill
Where we didn't have to March just to have a
place to belong
Where guns didn't end up in the wrong person's
hands
And now they have the blood of an innocent
Man
Where we didn't have to still fight for a seat at
the table
All because our skin isn't favored
Where we don't have people begging for more
All because of our system that is failing the poor
Where food insecurities, climate changes and
lack of jobs wouldn't create a political war
Where the haves and have nots can work
together
To build back up a country that isn't so lost.

boss up

I stand with my head held high
With my feet commanding the room
My presence alone
Says I'm no fool
I belong just like you
I'm a boss
How do you do
It's my time to shine
I've been holding back for way too long
But watch my next move
It's going to call you to follow through
Shine bright don't let no one dim your light
For you are a boss who's making real moves that
won't cause you to lose

in my skin

I am comfortable in my own skin
Beautiful dark skin
Beautiful brown skin
beautiful light skin
my melanin is sweet and beautiful
i don't have to fear the skin I'm in
my skin is natural and true
it's beautiful on the inside and out
it radiates love and pureness
my skin is who I am
I am beautiful deep within

focus

in uncertainty the vision is very clear
i can focus on what the task is at hand
i am not bewildered by things I cannot control
in plain view it's evident what I need to do
i know I am covered and worthy
but sometimes I have to try something new
it clear that some people just isn't for you
i am not unclear on what I need to do
i let it go like Frozen tells us to do
i'm focus on my vision
20/20 to be exact
i am determined to stay focus
on my task at hand
because what's in front of me
i don't have time to look back
it's clear that I am on the right track

presence

In this moment I will not be silent
My presence whether you like it or not is wanted
I am present in this moment
You can try to shut me down and kill my song
But I beat to my own drum
I am dancing like freedom just sung
You can't hold me back from speaking my truth
Because when it's all said and done
My presence will cut you up
You can't hold me back like a prisoner
Because the truth is my presence makes such
impression
It makes you question your own presence.